AF425670

Published by THRU the BIBLE Press
Designed by Fluid Communications, Inc.

PHILEMON, JAMES & JUDE

BIBLE COMPANION

THRU the BIBLE PRESS

READ THIS FIRST

This Bible Companion is a summary of Dr. J. Vernon McGee's teaching of the books of Philemon, James and Jude heard on THRU the BIBLE. These summarized lessons get to the heart of Bible passages and are intended to stir your own thinking, prayer, and study.

Begin with prayer. Dr. McGee said, "We are living in the day of the ministry of the Holy Spirit, the day of grace, when the Spirit of God takes the things of Christ and reveals them to us." Before you start each lesson, ask the Lord to use it to grow you up in grace and in the knowledge of our Lord and Savior Jesus Christ as He is revealed in that section. Dr. McGee said, "This is the secret of life and of Christian living."

As you study, read the Bible passage first. Invite God to open your eyes and deepen your understanding of His Word. That's a request God loves to answer!

If you want to listen to Dr. McGee's complete teaching on any specific passage, go to *TTB.org/Philemon, TTB.org/James* or *TTB.org/Jude*. The corresponding audio messages are listed at the top of the summaries. You can also use this Bible Companion to follow along and take notes while you listen to Dr. McGee teach a book of the Bible on the radio or online.

After every lesson, several questions are listed for your personal consideration or, if you're reading this as a group, for your discussion. Ask the Spirit to help you take to heart what He wants to show you.

TABLE OF CONTENTS

PHILEMON

BIBLE COMPANION

PHILEMON

 Begin with prayer

 Read Philemon

 Listen at *TTB.org/Philemon* to **Philemon**

In the Old Testament, God communicated through law, history, poetry, prophecy, and narratives, but now in the church age, He inspired letters—a new, more personal and direct method. Most of the letters were written to churches, but we have one personal letter, written from Paul to Philemon. Honestly, it feels like we're looking over Philemon's shoulder at his mail, but the Holy Spirit included this letter in Scripture for a very definite reason, and it's both inspired and important.

Behind this letter is a story, of course—a pretty dramatic one set against the backdrop of slavery. Philemon was a rich man living in Colosse, in modern-day Turkey. He owned many slaves, all subject to the whim of their master.

Apparently, Philemon knew Paul from Ephesus when Paul taught every day in the school of Tyrannus. Of the thousands of people who heard Paul teach over the two years there, Philemon was just one who came to a saving faith in the Lord Jesus.

Somewhere in Philemon's story, his slave, Onesimus, took a chance one day, as any slave would have done, and made a run for it. Onesimus made it all the way to Rome where he could get lost in the great population.

One day, Onesimus found out there was a slavery in freedom and there was a freedom in slavery. Imagine him going down a Roman road one day and seeing a group of people gathered around a teacher. The odd thing was the teacher was in chains. Onesimus had run away from chains, and he thought he was free. But when he listened to that man he thought, *That man's free, and I'm still a slave—to appetite, to the economy, to myself. But although he's chained, that man is free.*

After the others had drifted away, Onesimus asked Paul more about the gospel he was preaching, and soon a miracle happened in Onesimus' life and he was set free indeed. He put his trust in Christ and became a new creation in Christ Jesus.

Then this new man, Onesimus, confessed the things that were wrong in his life and which he wanted to make right—including his status as a runaway slave. They exchanged "small world" stories and realized that Paul knew Onesimus' master, Philemon. *"Should I go back to him?"* Onesimus wondered.

"Yes, Onesimus, you must go back, but you are going to go back to a different situation. I will send a letter with you."

And that's the letter we have in Scripture—the Epistle of Paul to Philemon. As we read over Philemon's shoulder, we see two purposes in its short pages. The first is a spiritual illustration of Jesus' love for us when he pleads our case before God. Paul's letter to Philemon is one of the best illustrations of Jesus' substitution for us. When Paul writes, "receive him as you would me. But if he has wronged you or owes anything, put that on my account" (vs. 17-18), we can hear Christ agreeing to take our place and to have all our sin imputed to Him. He took our place in death, but He gives us His place in life. We can stand like Christ does before God, or we have no standing at all. *"Give Onesimus the kind of welcome you'd give me,"* Paul asks.

The *practical* purpose in this letter is to teach brotherly love. In his other prison letters, Paul spoke of the new relationship between master and servant. Here he demonstrates how it should work. These men, belonging to two different classes in the Roman Empire, hating each other and hurting each other, are now brothers in Christ, and they are to act like it. The human heart has always had a great desire to be free. Now these two men were free to follow Christ, and it meant something unique to both of them.

JESUS
ASKS US
TO GO THE SECOND
MILE.
He is a
generous Lord.

THRU the BIBLE

About Onesimus. His name means "profitable," and Paul played with that meaning as he wrote to Philemon. As a slave, Onesimus wasn't very useful. His heart wasn't in his work, but now Paul is sending him back to Philemon as a believer, and he says, *"He is going to be profitable to you now. However, don't receive him as a slave. Take him back as a brother."*

About Philemon. Paul calls Philemon, "our beloved friend." Paul loved this man, and he is confident in asking this favor of him. If you write out a prayer list of the apostle Paul, be sure to put Philemon on that list. Every time Paul mentions his name, Paul is praying for him. Likely Philemon was a prominent person in his city, but more importantly, his life was a testimony to the Lord Jesus Christ. He loved the Lord, he refreshed God's people, and he was faithful to them both. He lived in responsive obedience, reverent and sensitive before God. He believed God to work in him what pleased Him (see Philippians 2:13).

About the favor. Paul writes Philemon to ask a favor. He's diplomatic, cautious, and loving and appeals to Philemon on a threefold basis:

- Please receive Onesimus as "a beloved brother" (i.e. don't punish him as a captured runaway slave).

- Do this "for love's sake"—our shared love as believers in Christ Jesus.

- Do this "for [me], the aged, and now also a prisoner of Jesus Christ." Paul was near the end of his life and had suffered and been persecuted as a missionary for Christ. In this letter, Paul doesn't call himself an apostle, but "a prisoner of Jesus Christ" (not a prisoner of Rome.) He can't come accompany Onesimus personally because he's in chains in Rome.

Paul is pleading on behalf of his "spiritual" son. He calls Timothy and Titus his sons, and now Onesimus. He admits Onesimus would have been helpful to him in Rome (prisoners needed outsiders to help with life's basic necessities). *"If you want to send him back to me, that will be all right."* Did Philemon send Onesimus back to Paul? Again, we don't know, but it's not a stretch to imagine that on the next boat returning to Rome, there was Onesimus carrying a lot of things to add to Paul's comfort.

Since Onesimus has become a believer, his status and relationship to Philemon are different. He is still a slave according to the Roman law, but he is more than that to Philemon. He is now a beloved brother.

Behind this beautiful letter is a grand illustration of what Jesus does for us. He pleads for us to the Father on our behalf as a sinner who trusts Christ as the Savior. *"Receive this sinner as You receive me, Father."* We have as much right to heaven as Christ has, for we have His right to be there.

Paul says, *"Since you count me as a partner, Philemon, receive Onesimus just like you would receive me. You always put me up in that fancy guest room. Don't send him out in the cold; put him up in the guest room, too."*

Paul continues, *"Look, if Onesimus stole something from you or did something wrong, just put it on my credit card."*

Do you see this glorious picture? When you came to God the Father for salvation, imagine the Lord Jesus Christ saying, "If he/she has wronged You or owes You anything, put it on My account." Christ on the cross paid off your debt created by your sin. He gave His life and shed His blood to pay our entire debt of sin. But that isn't all. Even then, you weren't fit for heaven, but the Lord Jesus says, *"If You count Me as Your Son, treat him/her as You would Me."* That's what it means to be in Christ—accepted in the Beloved. *"Put him/her in the nicest guest room."* That's how God the Father accepts us on behalf of the Lord's pleading for us.

We don't know how this situation worked out for Onesimus. Paul felt confident that Philemon will do even more than he requests, like any true believer would. Jesus asks us to go the second mile. He is a generous Lord. We should be generous people—even when wronged. Because that's when the light shines brightest in this dark world.

♥ FOR DISCUSSION AND REFLECTION

1. What does it tell us about the Apostle Paul that he was still preaching the gospel, even when he was chained and on house arrest?

2. Why would Paul tell Onesimus to go back to slavery, even though he had escaped?

3. How does the gospel level the ground between different groups of people, even slaves and masters?

4. The gospel changed Onesimus from being unprofitable to profitable. What are some ways the gospel has changed you?

5. Paul could have commanded Philemon with his authority as an apostle; instead, he pleaded with him to make a wise decision. Why do you think he chose this approach?

6. Onesimus' status changed from slave to brother. What are some ways that accepting Christ has changed your identity?

7. Imagine you were a companion of Paul's. Would you anticipate Onesimus returning to Philemon? Why or why not?

JAMES

BIBLE COMPANION

WHY DOES GOD TEST OUR FAITH?

 Begin with prayer

 Read **James 1:1-18**

 Listen at *TTB.org/James* to **James 1:1-3, James 1:3-11, James 1:3-13, James 1:13-15,** and **James 1:14-19**

Of all the books of the New Testament, the Epistle of James was written first, sometime between 45-50 A.D. Some say it was written to argue with Paul's book to the Thessalonians, but in fact, James wrote his book years before. He wrote this letter to the Jews, all twelve tribes who were scattered abroad. The early church was 100 percent Jewish in those early years.

Although James was Jesus' half-brother, he never refers to himself as such; instead, he calls himself Jesus' bondservant—His slave. Perhaps he never boasted about his relationship with Jesus because before the resurrection, James didn't believe Jesus' claims to be Messiah. Once he believed, however, he followed the Lord faithfully. In fact, James likely became head of the church at Jerusalem, and in Acts 15 he presided over the history-defining great council there.

James wrote this very practical letter to the Jews living abroad about what it means to walk by faith, specifically how we should be characterized by our good works. Faith prompted our salvation, but our works are the *result* of our salvation. God looks down and sees our hearts, and He knows whether we believe or not—that is justification by faith. But our neighbors next door don't see our hearts; they can only judge by our works, the *fruit* of our faith. James urges us to act on what we believe—to let God's Word inform the way we live. Tradition says his nickname was "Old Camel Knees" because he spent so much time in prayer.

The Epistle of James deals with the ethics of Christianity rather than doctrine. James bears down on some practical issues but weaves the theme of how faith produces these good works into every chapter. He talks about how to prove faith is real and illustrates some of the ways God tests faith.

"Count it all joy when you fall into various trials," he begins. Trouble will come, so don't think it strange that something terrible is happening to you. Instead, rejoice that God is testing you in this way. James isn't saying Christians will necessarily experience joy when we go through trials. Trials are meaningless, suffering is senseless, and testing is irrational unless there's some good purpose for them. God assures us there is (see Romans 8:28).

When you stand under the pressures, be alert to your heart's attitude toward your trouble. Believe that God has permitted this trial for a purpose. Be confident He is working something out in your life. You may not *understand* His purpose, but it pleases Him when you walk by faith and not by sight.

What are some of God's purposes in these tests of faith?

James urges us to let patience develop us into mature and well-developed Christians. Patience is the fruit of the Holy Spirit. You won't become patient by *trying* to be patient, but neither will the Holy Spirit deliver it on a silver platter. Patience comes through suffering and testing. Testing and trials produce patience in our lives so we might develop into full-grown children of God. This is so relevant to today!

God allows trouble so that we learn patience, which will then produce real hope and love in us. We'll also gain wisdom related to our trials if we ask Him for it.

Wisdom is the exercise and practical use of knowledge. Wisdom is knowing how to act under difficult circumstances, or when you face problems or questions. Life is filled with these situations, and we clearly need God's wisdom to navigate them. God is in the business of giving out wisdom "liberally"—that is, pure, simple giving of good without mixing in evil or bitterness. If you lack wisdom, go to God who will hear and answer your prayer. Just believe Him when He says He will help you.

Turn these problems over to Him. You don't have the brains to meet the problems of life, but you do have a heavenly Father who can supply the wisdom you need. Tomorrow you're going to be tempted to solve the problem yourself, but that's a mistake. When you're tempted to doubt God's purposes, turn the problem back over to Him. Start each day by giving Him your issues and trust Him that He'll give you the wisdom you need to face the challenges.

Rejoice today that you have a Savior who is not only going to save you for heaven—that's certainly good enough—but who will help you this very day. It doesn't matter if you are the humblest saint or the poorest person on earth; you are rich in Christ, and you have something to rejoice over.

The book of James is sometimes compared to the book of Proverbs, which is written like a college curriculum on wisdom. Here in the Epistle of James, we find a different school—the "School of Hard Knocks." God wants to bring His own to full Christian maturity. He tests His children to weed out the phonies and the fake saints and to assure His true children that He will help. Our trials are proof positive of our faith. If you are having trouble, that's a good sign you belong to Him. He also wants to produce patience in your life and confidence that God is working out His purpose in your life.

When faith is tested and surrounded by darkness, when the waves are rolling high and all seems lost, the child of God knows this is not the end. It may be gloom now, but it will be glory later on (see Psalm 30:5). James says someday the one who has suffered "will receive the crown of life which the Lord has promised to those who love Him."

James says the person who endures and overcomes in this kind of test (sometimes called a "temptation"), yet still believes God is allowing it for a definite reason, this Christian will be awarded "the crown of life."

Testing of any kind tends to create pessimism, bitterness, and cynicism; it's easy for people to get caught in the "why?" or "why me?" loop. But God tests us to grow our faith and develop our patience, and He has something very specifically in mind for the future.

People who have suffered a great deal often enjoy a closer, more loving relationship with the Lord Jesus Christ. Suffering causes them to look forward to the day when the Lord welcomes them into His presence, when He will reward them with the crown of life.

Scripture mentions a half dozen different crowns given as *rewards* to believers. The crown of life is a reward for those who endure trials in their lives, yet they still love the Lord. Testing will either drive you to the Lord or it will drive you away from Him. So many Christians become bitter when life gets hard. But keep thinking about the moment you will stand in the Lord's presence. Don't let the very thing your heavenly Father was using to develop your character and to bring you into a loving relationship with Him make you bitter. We will each endure trials, but if you emerge from them, still loving the Lord Jesus Christ, then there's going to be a reward waiting for you.

Someday you will stand before Jesus Christ—everyone will. If you do not know the Lord Jesus Christ as Savior, you will stand before God at the Great White Throne judgment that will determine your eternal destiny. If you do know Jesus Christ as your Lord and Savior, you will go beforehand to the Bema seat of Christ. Here, your life will be evaluated to determine rewards. It is here you will be awarded the crown of life which Jesus Himself offers to those who, after they have endured the testings of this life, *love* Him.

People often blame God for many things for which He is not responsible. Does God tempt you to do evil? James says no. God can't be tempted with evil, nor does He tempt with evil (vv. 13-14). God tests, He doesn't tempt. Jesus was tested to prove we have a Savior who could not sin. God cannot be tempted with sin, and God will not tempt you with sin. There is no evil in God. In Him all is goodness and all is light and all is right (see 1 John 1:5).

From the beginning of time, mankind has blamed God for his own faults and failures and filth. Remember the Garden of Eden? Adam blamed God for tempting him to sin, then he blamed the woman (whom God gave him), and then she blamed the serpent (see Genesis 3:12-13). But who causes you to sin? You choose it. Who draws you away to do evil? Who makes you yield to evil temptation? God doesn't. The devil doesn't. *You* are responsible. Every person is drawn in our own way to sin.

One person may be tempted to drink. Another may be tempted to overeat. Another may be tempted in the realm of sex. The problem is always within the individual. No outside influence can make us sin. The trouble is within us; it's our old nature. We may try to rationalize it away, but the Bible calls them *sins*. James says it's your own lust (an uncontrolled longing) that draws you away into sin. Our old nature joins with the outward temptation, and we act on it. On its own, temptation is not sin. But when sin in our hearts becomes an action, our fellowship with God is broken—and that is a death (see 1 John 1:6).

"Do not be deceived," James warns. The word "deceived" here means to wander or to stray, like the lost sheep the Lord Jesus said the shepherd went after. *"Don't wander. Don't think that somehow you can get by with sin."* If you have never been born again, you are a habitual and perpetual sinner who doesn't have a line of communication with God. If you can live in sin and enjoy it, you are not a child of God—it's just that simple.

Test your own heart today. Ask the Lord to show you if there's anything between Him and you (Psalm 139:23).

NEXT: What happens when you obey God's Word?

❤ FOR DISCUSSION AND REFLECTION

1. At the core of the book of James is the idea that genuine faith will produce good works. What works would you point to in your life which others might observe and conclude that you have faith?

2. Why do you think God might find it necessary to test a person's faith?

3. Our attitude matters a great deal when it comes to enduring trials. When a trial comes, is your initial reaction one of faith or something else?

4. The process which ends with wisdom begins with patience, but patience has to grow. Are there areas of your life where you are resisting growing in patience?

17

5. Wisdom is so important that we can never just rely on our own. Who do you know who has wisdom you can turn to when you need it?

6. Trials will come. What can you do before they arrive to help make sure they produce patience in your life rather than anger and bitterness?

7. James tells us that, when we sin, we have only ourselves to blame. He reminds us of Adam blaming God and then Eve for his sin. If you could ask Adam, what reason do you think he would give for blaming Eve?

EVERY GOOD GIFT

 Begin with prayer

 Read **James 1:19-27**

 Listen at *TTB.org/James* to ***James 1:19-22, James 1:22-25,*** *and* ***James 1:25—2:2***

It's been the custom down through the centuries to blame God for such things as tornadoes, earthquakes, and floods ("acts of God"). But if you have a *good* gift, it also came from Him. Count your many blessings today: The sunshine, the rain, the cloudy day, the bright day, the green grass, the water you drink, and the air you breathe. We really don't understand how good He is.

In fact, it's God's will that every person be born again—that's how good He is. It's our choice whether we are or not. When God's will joins with our will, we will be born again. When you willingly come to Him and believe His Word and accept Jesus Christ as your Savior, you will be born again.

And that's just the beginning. After we're saved, we need to be quick to hear the Word of God. This is how you will grow in your Christian life. You take something that is living, powerful, and sharper than any two-edged sword (see Hebrews 4:12) and then listen to the Spirit of God who indwells you and who wants to teach it to you. The Creator of this universe and the Redeemer of lost sinners wants to talk to you—so be alert and quick to listen.

James also tells the child of God to be "slow to speak." God gave us *two* ears and *one* mouth—there must be a very definite reason for that. Talking too much puts us in danger. Next, be "slow to wrath." Don't argue about stupid stuff. An uncontrolled temper wrecks your testimony. You may feel you are angry because you are defending the faith, but the wrath of man simply does not work with the righteousness of God. Don't kid yourself that you are angry for His sake, because He's not angry—He's in the saving business.

God is pleased when we leave the "filthiness" of the flesh behind us and instead receive with a humble spirit the Word of God, which is rooted in our hearts. This is the Word that introduced you to Jesus your Savior. It is also the Word that will keep you from sin. The Word has already brought salvation to you; now it shows you how to live as a Christian. Salvation is in three tenses: You have been saved, you are being saved, and you will be saved.

The child of God can never get away from the Word of God. Every child wants to hear his father's voice, especially if it's comforting. Correction is OK, too, when it's delivered with encouragement. If a Christian isn't interested in the Word of God or doesn't stay near it, they're going to get into trouble.

James really likes to get practical with faith issues. Prove yourself to be a "doer of the word," he says. Obey the Word, don't just listen to it without really pondering what it means. Don't fool yourself into thinking you're following God if you ignore what He says.

The Bible is different from any other book. You can read most books to gain information, knowledge, intellectual stimulation, spiritual inspiration, amusement, or entertainment. But the Word of God *demands action*.

A book about history asks nothing of you. You can read literature, but you'll have no imperatives, no declarations, and no explanations to follow. Science books make no demand on you whatsoever. A cookbook gives you a recipe, but it doesn't say you have to cook. However, the Word of God is a command. It is a trumpet, an appeal for action. Here's an example. John 3:36 says, "He who believes in the Son has everlasting life; and he who does not believe the Son shall not see life, but the wrath of God abides on him." The message of the Lord Jesus Christ is (1) "repent," (2) "come to Me," and (3) "believe" (see Matthew 11:28 and Mark 1:15). The Word of God demands belief.

God isn't asking anything of you until you become His child. But to those of us who have become children of God, He says, *do the Word.* God doesn't ask the unsaved person to do anything at all; He wants to tell them that *He* has done something. God just asks the unsaved person to believe.

But we who know Him should hear the Word of God and then go do it. God intends the Word to produce creative action in us and to make for practical application, exciting living, and a thrilling experience. If we are motivated by an inner desire and enjoy Spirit-filled living, we can enjoy life and all its thrills, and then enjoy Bible study equally as well—in fact, it will be thrilling to us.

We won't just hear the words, like we're just auditing the class. No, we'll be students of the Word. We'll take notes, go through exams, write papers, and be rewarded with a diploma. Faith leads to *action.*

It's too easy to fall into the trap of rationalizing our inaction and rationalizing our sin (see 1 John 1:8). Have you ever looked in a mirror, noticed the big glob of ketchup on your cheek, and then ignored it? James says if you don't do the Word, it's like you see a reflection of yourself in a mirror—the you as you really are—and yet do nothing about the flaws you see.

James says, in effect, *Take time in front of the mirror.* Give it your attention, be alert to the Word of God. Don't treat it casually. Instead, let God's Word remind you of Him and call you back into a relationship with Him.

God saves us by grace. He calls us to live in that grace, too. It's "the perfect law of liberty," James said. This isn't Moses' Law that other books of the Bible talk about. This is the law of faith and of love. The Lord said, "If you love Me, keep My commandments" (John 14:15), and John says in his first letter, "For this is the love of God, that we keep His commandments" (1 John 5:3).

When you drive down a freeway, you notice all the traffic. If anyone wants the freedom to drive down that freeway, they had better obey the laws. The freedom we have in Christ is in obeying His laws of love and faith and grace. If we love Him, we'll want to obey them. But His laws aren't hard or rigorous. Your freedom doesn't entitle you to break the Ten Commandments. Those laws are for the weak, for the natural man. Laws are for lawbreakers: What to do, where to go, and how, with a punishment prescribed for those who break over. Honest citizens don't need the law.

Today God has called His children to a higher level. A child of God has a spiritual spontaneity, a high and lofty motive, an inspiration of God. The believer has no desire to murder. He lives above the law. He is now motivated by the love of the Savior, and he wants to obey Him. The more we read and study the Word, the more we will learn, we will love, and we will live. Joy fills and floods the soul. We are not like galley slaves, whipped and chained to a bench and doing that which we don't want to do.

If we are to live for God, then we need to know His Word. As a healthy, growing child of God, you keep learning what pleases Him.

Next, James tells you a specific way to please the Lord—and it may not be what you think. James uses the words "religious" and "religion" more than any other New Testament writer. The word "religion" comes from a Latin word which means "to bind back." It means to go through a ritual or ceremony.

Many religions today have faithful, zealous followers. But Christianity is not a religion; it Is a person, and that person is Jesus Christ—you either have Him or you don't have Him. James says to live a pure life before God means to live out the Word. That's the kind of religion that pleases the Lord. Christianity certainly ought to produce this kind of compassion and mercy. We need to practice a "religion of the street" where we are in contact with the world in a personal way, with tenderness and kindness and helpfulness.

But contact with the world doesn't mean we should act like the world or let its ugly mark rub off on us. As believers, we are *in* this world but we are not *of* this world. Go ahead and touch those around you with love and kindness and grace, but be careful not to be sucked into its mold. You belong to Jesus.

**NEXT: What genuine faith looks
like in the life of a believer.**

❤ FOR DISCUSSION AND REFLECTION

1. Most Christians know they need to be immersed in the Word of God, but that doesn't mean it is easy to do. What do you need to change or do differently to be in the Word more than you are right now?

2. Being slow to speak isn't just a matter of verbalization, it has to be a change in mentality. And most of us find talking comes more naturally than listening. Who do you know who is a good listener? What can you learn from them?

3. Are there any practical steps you can take to put the command to be "slow to anger" into practice?

4. What does it look like for a person to be a "doer of the Word?"

5. One of the reasons we struggle to apply the Bible's teachings is that we have no process for doing so. What are some principles for you to use when applying the Bible?

6. What are some ways we can be more attentive to the voice of the Holy Spirit when we are in God's Word?

7. If you could go back and ask James, "In one sentence, what is the difference between a religion and Christianity?", what do you think his answer would be?

25

The Creator of this universe and the Redeemer of lost sinners wants to talk to you—

so be alert and quick to listen.

THRU the BIBLE

FAITH ALIVE

 Begin with prayer

 Read **James 2**

 Listen at *TTB.org/James* to ***James 2:1-13*** *and* ***James 2:14-26***

Both poverty and riches can be a curse. Proverbs 30:8 says, *Give me neither of them.* What then is God's solution to the problem of poverty?

God's war on poverty and riches does not march under the banner of the dollar, where millions are appropriated for relief. And it is not aimed primarily at the head or at the stomach, but at the heart. This is a war against class.

In this section, James talks about distinctions and divisions among believers brought about by money. *Don't say you love Jesus Christ and be a spiritual snob*, he says. *All believers are your family in the body of Christ, whatever their denomination.* There is a fellowship of believers— the rich, the poor, the common people, the high, the low, the bond and free, the Jew and the Gentile, the Greek and the barbarian, male and female. We are *one* when the Lord Jesus Christ is the common denominator. Friendship hangs over us like a banner.

Friendship and fellowship are the legal tender among believers. If you belong to the Lord Jesus Christ and another person belongs to the Lord Jesus Christ, he is your brother. Furthermore, if a sinner comes into your church or you otherwise come into contact with him, remember he is a human being for whom Christ died. He stands at the foot of the cross, just as you do.

Some people walk into church in fine clothes and lots of bling. They look like peacocks strutting their stuff. Others come in with torn, shabby clothing. James contrasts these two people at the extremes of the social ladder. Be careful not to tell the poor man to stand up in the rear and put the peacock down in front. Don't be partial in yourselves or act like a judge discerning motives. Who knows if the poor believer may be the most spiritually rich person in that church?

God has made it very clear from Genesis to Revelation that He has a special concern and consideration for the poor. They have been despised by the world. Their only hope is in Jesus Christ. When you mistreat the poor, you are blaspheming the name of Christ.

If you want to please God, obey Him and act responsibly. James makes it very clear what you are to do: "Love your neighbor as yourself."

Moses' Law condemns discriminating between the rich and poor. Some will say, "Well, at least I didn't commit murder or adultery." But James writes that we are guilty of breaking the commandments no matter which one it is that we broke. We all stand before God as lawbreakers.

The Lord Jesus said, "If you love Me, keep My commandments…. This is My commandment, that you love one another as I have loved you" (John 14:15; 15:12).

In addition to how we treat each other, God also tests us by our works, our actions. For generations, Bible teachers have argued that James' discussion of good works contradicts the apostle Paul's assertion that faith alone can save you (Galatians 2:16). But James and Paul are in perfect agreement; they are discussing the same subject from different viewpoints. They stand back-to-back, fighting opposite foes.

In that day, some religious people said you had to come to the Law to be saved. Paul answered that by saying only faith in Christ can save you. *Saving faith*—a faith which is genuine and real—will transform a person's life. If it doesn't, it was just an empty faith. James says the faith which saves you will produce works of faith. The faith that doesn't produce good works is phony and counterfeit. *Doing* follows *believing*. As John Calvin put it, "Faith alone saves, but the faith that saves is not alone."

James says the works you do are the fruit of your faith. Paul talks about the root of faith being Jesus alone; you can't ever be good enough to work your way into heaven. In spite of their different focuses, both Paul and James say that faith alone saves and saving faith shows up in your life by good works. This is faith alive!

You can tell when faith is genuine, just look at someone's life. James gives the practical illustration of a phony Christian who meets someone in need—whether it be for food or clothing. They bless the needy person with flowery words but send them on their way still naked and hungry. What good is that? There must be a vocation to go along with the vocabulary. You can say pious words and sound very spiritual, but unless you follow through with action, it means nothing. A living faith *produces* something—you can *identify* it.

You cannot say you are a child of God and live completely unto yourself. Let your actions speak for you. You are telling by your life whether your faith is genuine or not. Lip service is not the evidence of saving faith—even the demons believe. Saving faith produces living faith. Without evidence of a changed life, your faith is empty and futile, as far as the world is concerned.

James gives two illustrations of this from familiar Old Testament people.

Remember Abraham? (Of course, they would.) Both the apostle Paul and Genesis say that Abraham was saved by faith (see Genesis 15:6; 22:1-14). Was Abraham justified when he offered his son Isaac? *Did* he offer his son Isaac? No. Then what was Abraham's work of faith? His faith caused him to lift that knife to do a thing which he didn't believe God would ever ask him to do. But since God had asked him, he was willing to do it. He believed God would raise Isaac from the dead. Abraham never actually offered Isaac, because God provided a substitute, but he would have done it if God had not stopped him. What saved Abraham? He believed God.

The second person James described was Rahab, known as "the harlot"—hardly someone you would consider "religious." But Rahab also believed God and this faith saved her, as she proved with her actions. Rahab lived on the walls of Jericho at the time when the Israelite spies were planning on attacking the city. Rahab received the spies, hid them from her own people, then told them how to escape without being detected (see Joshua 2 and Hebrews 11:31). She turned her back on her old life and did something. She said in effect, *I will hide you because I believe God is going to give the people of Israel this land. We have been hearing about you for forty years, and I believe God.* She was justified before God by her faith. However, before her own people and before the Israelites, she was justified by works.

Faith is the root, and the root produces the kind of fruit that the root itself is. If you have the root of a plum tree, it will grow and produce plums. If you have a living faith in God, you will produce godly fruit in your life. Faith without works is like a dead body in a morgue. But faith alive shows us in whom you believe.

NEXT: What our words say about us.

♥ FOR DISCUSSION AND REFLECTION

1. Applying James' words about friendship and fellowship means putting effort into relationships with other members of God's family. Who do you think the Holy Spirit might be leading you to pursue a relationship within the body of Christ?

2. Are a person's economic status and their level of spiritual maturity related? Why or why not?

3. Why are members of the family of God so susceptible to the temptation to discriminate against others, even fellow believers?

4. Given what James has taught about the relationship of good works and faith, what does the presence of discrimination in the body of Christ say about our faith?

5. What does the example of Abraham teach us about living a life of faith we can implement in our own lives?

6. Rahab may not be the first person who comes to your mind when you think of examples of faith, but James points to her as a prime example. What does Rahab's faith show us about God's grace?

7. If you were James, would you have used Rahab as an example in your letter? Why or why not?

JAMES

7. If you were James, would you have used Rahab as an example in your letter? Why or why not?

33

Faith alone saves, and saving faith shows up in your life by good works. This is faith alive!

GOD BUGS YOUR CONVERSATION

 Begin with prayer

 Read **James 3**

 Listen at *TTB.org/James* to *James 3:1-4* and *James 3:5-18*

God has the right to bug, or listen in on, our conversations. He has had that right for a long time and has heard everything you have ever said. The average person says about 30,000 words every day. That's a decent length book. In a lifetime, we could fill a library with our words.

This is just one of the ways God tests if our faith is genuine. Previously we've studied how God watches how we act when we're going through trials, how we treat people, especially the poor, and how much our lives blossom with good works. All this is evidence of saving faith.

James now has quite a bit to say about the use and abuse of the tongue—the words we say and what they say about us.

James has already told us he was going to get to this. In James 1:26 he said that if anyone thinks he's religious yet can't control what he says, then he's fooling himself. James also told us we have two ears, and God gave them to us so we can hear twice as much as we can say.

The tongue is the most dangerous weapon in the world. More deadly than the atom bomb, no one makes a careful inspection of it. Someone has put it like this: "Thou art master of the unspoken word, but the spoken word is master of you." Once you have said them, they are beyond your control.

Teachers should be especially mindful of this because they have a greater responsibility in that they are in grave danger of teaching the wrong thing. Listen up, those who teach God's Word: God will judge us for what we teach and the way we teach. The more opportunity you have to give out the Word of God, the greater is your responsibility to God Himself.

We all stumble and fail, but the mature, godly person is "able also to bridle the whole body." In other words, if he can control his speech, he can control his entire body—in fact, his whole life. The tongue lifts man from the animal world. A person can put thought into words; he can express himself; he can be understood; he can communicate on the highest level. The tongue is a badge we wear—it identifies us. It is the greatest index to life, the table of contents of our lives.

James will first deal with the unbridled and unrestrained tongue. Just imagine if everything you said this past month was recorded and shared with the world. Now you're ready to listen to the various ways James describes someone who doesn't have control over what they say.

First, James describes how to control your speech like a horse being controlled by a bridle in its mouth. The bridle bits are not big, but they can hold a high-spirited horse in check and keep him from running away.

Large ships are also controlled by a little rudder that few people even see. A fierce storm may drive a ship, but a little rudder can control it. The tongue can also change the course of our lives. People have been ruined by gossip.

The tongue is more dangerous than a runaway horse or a storm at sea. The tongue is like the one little animal no zoo has in captivity, no circus can make it perform, no man can tame it. Only a regenerate tongue in a redeemed body, a tongue that God has tamed, can be used for Him.

The tongue is like a spark that lights a forest fire. Our words can burn through a church, burn through a community, burn through a town, and even burn through a nation. It might be little, but it can defile the whole body.

Of course, fire has been one of the greatest friends of man and nature. Some historians say civilization began when man discovered fire. When it is under control, it warms our bodies, it cooks our food, and it generates power to turn the wheels of industry. When it's under control, fire is a blessing; when it is out of control, it is devastating. It can be a cure, or it can be a curse.

You remember how Simon Peter's tongue betrayed him? On the night before Jesus went to the cross, Peter spoke affirming words to the Lord, and later that night he denied he knew Him. But on the Day of Pentecost, what was it the Lord used? It was Simon Peter's blundering, stumbling, bumbling tongue. He was a man set on fire for God.

Isn't it interesting that Romans 10:9 says that to be saved we are to confess the Lord Jesus *with our mouths* and believe *in our hearts* that God raised Jesus from the dead? In other words, our tongues and our hearts are to sing a duet in tune. Even the Lord Jesus Himself says our mouths will speak whatever the heart is full of (Matthew 12:34). What is in the heart will come out sooner or later.

With our words, we can both praise God or blaspheme God. We can be two-faced, double-minded, and forked-tongued. We can say both good and bad. James reminds us that no fountain on this earth will give both sweet and bitter water, nor will a tree bear both figs and olives. But our words can also reveal genuine faith. We testify for God. We can speak wisdom. That is, if our hearts are right with God.

If we aren't right with God, our words can stir up bitterness. James contrasts the tongue of the foolish believer and the tongue of the wise believer. First, it's important to note that an uncontrolled tongue raises the question whether or not a person even is a child of God. Can a genuine believer curse six days a week and then sing on the worship team on Sunday? Can he tell dirty jokes all week at work and then teach about the love of Jesus to a Sunday school class? Your tongue can do either one, but if it does both, it will stir up strife. A lying tongue is one that denies the Lord during the week by its conversation.

This kind of strife isn't from God but is "earthly, sensual, demonic"— and it's confusing. Scripture makes it very clear God isn't the author of confusion. The confusion we find in the world today is brought about by the work of the devil who uses our little tongues to cause so much trouble. The wickedness of the world is not merely human, it's human plus the evil supernatural from below, causing divisions and strife in our homes and churches. This is pure worldliness, as we'll discover in our next study. Worldliness in the church produces the cults, denominations, factions, divisions, and cliques. It fosters a spirit of rivalry and jealousy. This is "earthly"—that is, it is confined to the earth. It is "sensual"—that is, psychological. And then it's demonic.

"But the wisdom that is from above is first *pure*"—that is, it's not mixed or diluted. It comes directly from God. It's "peaceable, gentle, willing to yield, full of mercy and good fruits, without partiality and without hypocrisy." These are the fruits of faith. Works of faith develop meekness or humility, and humility leads to submission. You cannot have peace without this righteous chain.

How do we discern genuine faith in the Lord Jesus Christ? We've learned that *saving faith* produces good works and perseverance through trials, and it also affects how we treat people and how to control what we say. These all clearly point to genuine faith, obvious in the life of someone who follows Jesus Christ.

NEXT: The solution to worldliness and war.

❤ FOR DISCUSSION AND REFLECTION

1. Why do you think James spends so much time talking about the tongue and the danger of using it for evil?

2. How can our ability to control our tongues show our maturity in Christ?

3. Think about the words you have spoken over the last week. What have the words you have spoken told the listener about the condition of your heart?

4. Why should teachers pay special attention to the words of James about the tongue?

5. James talks about a sinful tongue being "unrestrained." What are some practical ways you can restrain your tongue?

6. How can we tell if the words we want to say are spiritual or earthly?

7. If you were the one writing the book of James, would you have
    written this much on the tongue? Why or why not?

41

THIS IS WAR

 Begin with prayer

 Read **James 4**

 Listen at *TTB.org/James* to **James 3:14—4:4** and **James 4:5-17**

What is worldliness?

Some say worldliness is a matter of how you entertain yourself. What kind of movies you go to, if you drink, etc. The book of James wouldn't agree.

Others say worldliness is the kind of crowd you run with. If you are with a worldly crowd who engages in these things, then you are worldly. Or is it the way you dress? The words you say? If you learn to throw in "Praise the Lord" and "Hallelujah" at the right times, perhaps you're not so worldly.

The worldly person must be the one who wants to make money to the exclusion of all else and who neglects the church. Or maybe the worldly person doesn't go to church at all but spends their Sundays on the golf course, fishing, boating, or watching their favorite team play baseball.

None of these define worldliness. They may not be good practices and might be sins of the flesh—but they're not worldliness. They may be symptoms of the disease, but nobody ever died of symptoms—they die of the disease. These are simply evidence of the deeper, actual problem.

James, the writer of this letter, says worldliness is strife and envy which produce "confusion and every evil thing" (3:16). And what do these produce? Wars and fighting. Big, global conflict as well as that little skirmish you had at church last week. You wanted to have your own way. So did they. The "desires for pleasure that war in your members" speak to the overwhelming demands of the members of your body for satisfaction.

James makes it very clear: Selfish desires lead to war. What James describes here is the spirit of the world. This spirit of strife is worldliness, and it represents your old nature. When the spirit of the world gets into the church, you have a worldly church. It may be bad on the global battlefield, but it's just as bad inside some churches and inside some hearts.

The dog-eat-dog competition in the business world—worldliness. Political parties split, and one group is pitted against another—worldliness. As capital and labor meet around the conference table—worldliness. In the social world, some climbers on the social ladder step on the hands of others. In your neighborhood, one family doesn't speak to another. Then this same spirit gets into the church. *That* is worldliness.

So what is the cure for this disease of worldliness? Surprisingly, it's prayer. It's expressing your faith in God. The apostle John says it's our continuing, persistent faith in Jesus the Son of God that is the victory that conquers and overcomes the world (see 1 John 5:4). The answer is to trust God absolutely, go to Him in prayer and commit to Him what's on your heart. When you find strife and envy there, talk to Him about it.

Many of us go to the Lord to tell Him how good we are, but that doesn't help anything. Tell Him where you need help, don't ask Him for something selfish. If all you want is your own way, flirting with the world every chance you get, you end up with God as your enemy. This is the way the world works: Take by force what you want, by hook or by crook lay hold of it, be envious and jealous of other folk, and cause strife.

James says the solution to the problem of worldliness is to go to the Lord Jesus and tell Him about our problem, tell Him everything. God is overloaded with grace. We can't even fathom the depth of His grace.

Grace has been defined as unmerited favor, but it's really love in action. God didn't save us by love, He saved us by grace. He has so much of it. God gives abundant grace—but we must carry it around in a humble container. We also must be ready to submit to Him.

When you go to a doctor for medical care, you submit yourself to him. Submit yourself also to God. We are surrounded by evil influences. We can't resist the devil in our own strength. Temptation, as we have seen, is on every hand. But God supplies His grace as needed, and His supply never runs out. *"This is yours,"* God says. *"You are to lay hold of it."*

God is a gentleman. He only comes as far as the door of your heart. He knocks, and you have to let Him in. But draw near to Him and He will draw near to you. When you've sinned, get clean again by confession and repentance. If you've been unfaithful, get your heart made true once more. Don't ever treat sin lightly. Mourn over your sin.

The devil will not get to you unless you get too far away from God. A wolf never attacks a sheep as long as it is with the rest of the sheep and with the shepherd. And the closer the sheep is to the shepherd, the safer it is. Our problem is that we get too far from God.

Humble yourself before the Lord, and He will lift you up. *He* will. Too often we think *we are* smart or strong or skilled. We think *we* are good enough, but God says we have no good in us. Nothing in us attracts Him but only our great need draws Him to us. If we are willing to humble ourselves and get down where He can lift us up, He will.

Don't bad-mouth each other; don't act like you're the judge. If you judge your brother, you put yourself above the law and treat it with contempt. Seriously, who do you think you are? When you talk about your brother, you put yourself in God's place.

Two types of people seek to take the position of God. One is the sinner who says, "I'm good enough to be saved. Lord, I don't need your salvation. You just move over and I'll sit beside you. I am my own savior." Then there's the other one who sits in judgment on everyone else. James says judgment is God's business (see also John 5:22). We are to judge ourselves and go to God in humility.

We also like to make big plans for the future, but James reminds us we don't know what tomorrow holds.

Human life lived apart from and without God is the most colossal failure in God's universe. Many of us never learn to really live down here on earth. Good thing our lives are in God's hand. We can't brag about a thing. We even mess up and don't even know it. If you know you should do a certain thing or help a certain cause—and you do not do it, *that* is sin.

Our lives are brief. Let's not spoil it with strife and envy. Come to Jesus Christ, put your life down before Him, and really start living. He wants to give you a life that's out of this world.

NEXT: What the Bible has to say about the rich and the poor.

♥ FOR DISCUSSION AND REFLECTION

1. Worldliness is a desire in our heart for things that are not of God. What might worldliness produce in our lives?

2. How can strife and envy in our hearts play out in our actions?

3. Why do we fail to take our problems to Jesus in prayer?

4. If grace is love in action, who are some people you need to show grace to?

5. The way to resist temptation is to submit to God. What are some ways you can intentionally submit to God in your life?

6. Do you know anyone who is an example of humility in your life? How can you follow their example?

7. Think about what life was like in the first century. Do you think worldliness is more of a temptation now, back then, or is it the same? Why?

God supplies His
grace as needed,
and His supply
never runs out.

RICH MAN, POOR MAN

 Begin with prayer

 Read **James 5**

 Listen at *TTB.org/James* to *James 5:1-6* and *James 5:5-20*

Being rich isn't the problem. But neither does being poor make you more godly. The lesson isn't in the coin, it's the heart, says James. The Bible doesn't condemn money—only the love of it (see 1 Timothy 6:10).

In the Roman world of James' day, there was no middle class. There was only the filthy rich and the filthy poor. Most of the Christians came from the very poor and slave classes.

James addresses now our wrong relationship to money, how we get it, and what we do with it after we've got it. The Lord Jesus Christ had a great deal to say about money. He taught three parables which help illustrate James' point.

Jesus tells the story of the poor man, Lazarus the beggar, who sat at the rich man's gate and what happened when they both died. In another parable, the Lord Jesus told about a rich man who hoarded his money, built big barns, and never gave a thought about eternity. The Lord called him a fool. In Jesus' third parable, the unjust steward teaches us that God holds us responsible not only for how we make money but also for how we spend it.

When James talks about money, he warns the rich to see money properly—a lesson appropriate for every generation. The rich of James' day lost all their wealth when the Romans destroyed Jerusalem in A.D. 70, just a couple decades after they received this letter from James.

But at Jesus' second coming, all of the world's wealth will mean nothing anyway. Regardless, riches are uncertain in any age. You always face a danger of a panic, a crash, a drought, or a depression. This is the way it's been since people started minting money.

"Don't you know that your silver and gold are going to rust?" Why? Because *we* are going to rust out, too. Death separates a rich man from his money. God gave us wealth to be dispersed, not hoarded.

Just like in Jesus' parables, James condemns the godless rich not only for hoarding money but for making it in a dishonest way. They robbed the poor to get rich. They made their riches by stepping on the hands of those beneath them (see also Proverbs 22:7). But be assured, God may do nothing about this now, but He says you are a fool. If you've decided to live for this life only, be sure to live it up now, because He will judge you in the future.

There's a lesson here for the rich man who is a Christian. How big is your bank account? If Jesus should come right now, would you be willing to let Him look into your safety deposit box? He'll do that someday. How are you making use of your riches? Just remember that riches never bring mankind happiness.

The Word of God has a lot to say about when Jesus Christ sets up His kingdom on earth. The poor are going to get a right and honest deal for the first time in history. All of the prophets emphasized this (see Isaiah 11:4 as an example). Christ Himself made it clear in the Sermon on the Mount (which will be the law of His kingdom) that He intends to give the poor a square deal under His reign (see Matthew 6:19-24).

Today, no political party will surprise us with a good deal for the poor. You can't look to mankind, to people who grasp for power and money, and expect them to act righteously. Our only hope is in Jesus Christ. *"Be patient. The harvest is coming,"* James says.

Throughout Scripture we are taught we should live in the light of the coming of Christ. James tells us to get our affairs straightened out before He comes, because if we don't, He will. This is a good word to each of us.

"Look at the prophets," James says. They are an example to us in how they were patient even in suffering. Job was an impatient man, but he learned patience. At the end of Job's trial, you'll see he learned a great lesson about how compassionate and generous the Lord was with him.

Since the Lord is compassionate, let your promise to Him be like an oath—like you were in a courtroom and swore an oath to tell the truth. All your conversation with others ought to be like that.

And speaking of conversations, your prayer life with God ought to have great passion and enthusiasm, too. James was a great man of prayer. He was nicknamed, "Old Camel Knees" because, having spent so much time on his knees in prayer, his knees were calloused.

"What do you do when someone is sick among you?" James asks. Call for the elders of the church and let them pray over him. That's the first thing. Then they are to anoint him with oil in Jesus' name. James is practical—get some medicine, then get people to pray. The prayer of faith will save the one who is sick, and the Lord will raise him up. And if he has committed sins, he will be forgiven.

We are to confess our sins to God and our faults to each other. If you have injured someone, then you ought to confess that to them. But confess your sins only to the Lord. First John 1:9 says, "If we confess our sins [to God], He is faithful and just to forgive us our sins and to cleanse us from all unrighteousness." Man cannot forgive sins; neither can any clergyman forgive sins—only God can do that.

But man's prayers can do a lot. The prayer of a person living right with God is powerful. Another great man of prayer, Elijah, a regular guy just like any of us, prayed hard that it wouldn't rain, and it didn't for three and a half years. Elijah wasn't a superhero; he was just like us, but he prayed with passion, and God answered him.

Then as a closing thought, James asked them if they knew an unsaved person who had not yet come to the truth. Don't write them off. Go after them. It doesn't matter if they're blatant, obvious sinners. When they come to a saving knowledge of Christ, their sins—though they be great—will be covered by the blood of Christ. The wonder of justification by faith is that once God has pardoned our sins, they are gone forever—removed from us as far as the east is from the west.

This is a wonderful conclusion for this very practical Epistle of James.

♥ FOR DISCUSSION AND REFLECTION

1. What would a good relationship to money look like for the Christian?

2. If God intends for money to be used as a tool, not hoarded, what are some specific ways you can use your money for the kingdom of God?

3. How can our use of money show our level of spiritual maturity and priorities?

4. Should we just wait for Jesus' return to one day treat the poor appropriately, or are there things we should be doing now to minister to those in poverty?

5. Jesus' example of compassion is all too often ignored. Who are some people you need to show compassion to, even if it is hard?

6. Many times, it is easier to confess our sins to God than those we have sinned against. Why is that, and is there anyone to whom you need to confess?

7. If you could go back and ask James why he ended his epistle talking
   about pursuing unsaved people who needed the truth, what do you
   think his answer would be?

55

JAMES

7. If you could go back and ask James why he ended his epistle talking
   about pursuing unsaved people who needed the truth, what do you
   think his answer would be?

JUDE

BIBLE COMPANION

WARNING SIGNS OF A FAITH GONE BAD

 Begin with prayer

 Read **Jude 1—4**

 Listen at *TTB.org/Jude* to *Jude Intro, Jude 1—3,* and *Jude 3, 4*

The short epistle of Jude is like a burglar alarm. Apostates have broken into the church through the side door when no one was watching. They're teaching against grace and against Jesus Christ.

In this short letter, Jude lights up the red alarm on the dangerous pronouncement that Jesus Christ's church is facing. In just 25 short verses, he describes in vivid and awe-inspiring language the frightful conditions coming for the church. The little prophecy of Jude affords a fitting introduction to the next book of Revelation.

Jude, the writer of this epistle, is the half-brother of the Lord Jesus Christ. James, another sibling, wrote the epistle of James and was identified by the apostle Paul as one of the pillars in the church at Jerusalem. They both introduce themselves as "a bondservant of Jesus Christ." Why don't you think they capitalized on their blood relationship with Jesus? Perhaps it's because neither of them believed Jesus' claim to be the Messiah until after His resurrection. It took Jesus rising from the dead for them to believe their half-brother was Messiah. When addressing this letter, Jude calls himself "a bondservant of Jesus Christ." The Resurrection changed everything for him.

Studying the short letter of Jude is like working a gold mine. All the rich nuggets are here for the mining. Jude originally intended to write on the theme of our salvation, but the Spirit of God put up a red warning sign and instructed him to instead call attention to the days of apostasy that would be coming. Jude then focused on what we should believe during the days when false teaching would take hold of the church.

He begins his letter to the saints by referring to them as "sanctified by God the Father," or better translated, "to those who by God the Father have been loved and are in a state of being the permanent objects of His love, and who for Jesus Christ have been guarded and are in a permanent state of being carefully watched, to those who are called ones."

This is a wonderful passage of Scripture. We are beloved by God the Father and preserved for Jesus Christ. The word "preserved" is the key to the book of Jude. As he writes about the apostasy that invades the church, Jude doesn't just warn or inform us, but he assures us of God's love and protection. We are kept in Jesus Christ (used four times). He is the one who keeps us from falling. God still says He is able to keep His own. He gives assurance of salvation to the believer even in the dark days of apostasy (see also Jude 21, 24). We have no merit or power to overcome the Evil One. The only way we are going to overcome is by the blood of the Lamb. Our sure salvation rests in Him. It is up to each of us whether or not we believe Him.

Jude also says that not only are we preserved in Jesus Christ, safe in Him, but we are also called. The word "called," as it is used in Scripture, is not only an invitation, but it's an invitation that is sent out, accepted, and made real because of the Spirit of God (see 1 Corinthians 1:22-24).

Our salvation highlights three precious words: "Mercy, peace, and love be multiplied to you." In addition to the strong relationship between them, these three words have subtle differences.

Love is an attribute of God's character. Because He is love, He is merciful and has provided grace. God's love encompasses all mankind. He doesn't want any to perish (see John 3:16). Today He loves every human being on this earth. He has no favorites. He treats all His creatures alike.

If you knew how much God loves you, it would break your heart and make you cry. You can keep from experiencing God's love, but you cannot keep Him from loving you. You can't keep the sun from shining, but you can put up an umbrella to keep the sun from shining on you. And there are certain umbrellas you can put up to keep from experiencing the love of God: The umbrella of resistance to His will, the umbrella of sin in your life, etc.

Although God loves you, He did not save you by love. God has other attributes: He is holy, He is righteous, He is just. He simply cannot let down the bars of heaven and, by lowering His standards, bring you in. He cannot do that any more than a human judge can uphold the laws of the land and yet accept a bribe under the table for letting a criminal off. If he does that, he is a crooked judge. If God did that with human beings, He is no better than a crooked judge. But God maintains His holiness and His righteousness and His justice. How? He provided His Son as the substitute. Now God, on a righteous basis, can save a sinner if he will come to Him and accept His salvation. This is called the grace of God. (See Ephesians 2:8-9.)

The *grace* of God, not the love of God, connects with the sins of men. God provided a Savior who paid the penalty for sins. On the basis of grace, God saves sinners.

However, sin has brought tragedy to the human family. We often hear the question: How can a loving God permit cancer? Disease and death came to the human family as consequences of sin. God sees the misery sin has caused, and the mercy of God goes out to man. He is rich in mercy. If you come to Him as a sinner and accept His salvation, He will save you by grace. Then, because He is rich in mercy, He will extend His mercy to you. He will help you and bring comfort to you at that time. You can trust Him in your time of need. A sinner needs the grace of God and a whole lot of mercy.

Think of it: We must be forgiven before we can be blessed. God must pardon before He can heal. We must be justified before we can be sanctified. In the order of the manifestation of God's purposes of salvation, the grace of God must go before and take away and make way for the mercy of God.

The "peace" of God is that experience which comes to the heart that is trusting Christ (see Romans 5:1). Peace with God is to know God is not difficult to get along with. He is not making it hard for us to be in fellowship with Him. He wants us to know He hasn't anything against us now that we know we are sinners and have trusted Christ as our

Savior. The world may point its finger at you and reject you, but God has accepted you. He loves you, and He wants to give you that peace so that at night you can pillow your head on God's promises.

Now that we have the confidence of God's peace, grace, and mercy, Jude sets before us the reason he is sounding the alarm and calling us to fight for the faith.

Certain people are out to destroy this peace, grace, and mercy, he points out. Other biblical writers have sounded the warning about apostates before Jude. *"I'm not telling you something new—others have written of this also and have warned you of that which is coming."*

"For certain men have crept in unnoticed." "Crept in" is an interesting phrase in the Greek language. It means "to enter alongside" or "to get in by the side, to slip in a side door." This is the way the apostates have come into the church. They came in by professing one thing and believing another. They did not come in the front door, declaring their doctrinal position. (See also 2 Corinthians 11:13-15; Acts 20:29-31; 2 Timothy 3:5-6.) They only pretended to believe the truth about God and pretended to be sound in the faith.

The acid test of any movement is what they believe about the person of Jesus Christ. If they deny He is God, you can rule them out immediately. But be careful. There are many ways they can deny the deity of Christ and yet give the impression they actually believe in Him as the Savior of the world (see 2 Peter 2:1 and Galatians 2:4). They are ungodly, meaning they simply leave God out of their lives. It's important to evaluate whether or not the person who teaches and preaches God's Word is godly.

By nature, ungodly men do two things: (1) They distort and deny the grace of God— turning it into an immoral freedom and treating it as an opportunity to do whatever they want. And (2) they deny that Jesus Christ is God.

Gross immorality characterizes the apostasy of our day. Many so-called Christian leaders have thrown overboard all of the great precepts of Scripture concerning morality. The immorality we now witness is marked by an arrogant recklessness of justice. Marriage is flouted and considered unessential. You may live with whomever you wish to live with in total disregard of the morality which builds homes and thereby builds a nation. Are they teaching a loose morality? Jude warns us to be on our guard against that.

An apostate is also characterized by a denial of our Lord Jesus Christ as God. He will talk about God and the Lord Jesus, but he denies who and what they actually are.

In Jude's day the apostasy was Gnosticism, which taught that the body was essentially evil and the spirit alone was good. Gnostics taught you are completely free to satisfy your lusts and do whatever you want, even if that means you practice blatant immorality, shameless sin, and arrogantly and proudly flout that sin publicly. They didn't understand grace and perverted it from the rich life God intended for His followers to live.

NEXT: This is how you can spot an apostate.

LESSON 1
♥ FOR DISCUSSION AND REFLECTION

1. Why do you think James and Jude, half-brothers of Jesus, did not believe in Him until after the Resurrection?

2. How can the knowledge that we have been preserved by God, and nothing will ever change that, change the way we think about ourselves?

3. What do you think is God's purpose in allowing dark days of apostasy to come?

4. If God loves us so much, why couldn't He just let us into heaven? And what does your answer tell us about who God is?

65

5. Peace with God through Jesus isn't just a feeling, it is something tangible, a reality that we experience. How aware are you of that peace, and what can you do to experience it more completely?

6. If false teachers attempt to slip in unnoticed, part of what we should do as a community is keep our eyes open for one another. Who helps you watch for false teaching, and who do you help watch out for?

7. Imagine you were a first century Christian tasked by Jude with preparing some questions to verify the truthfulness of what people believed about Jesus. What are some of the questions you would have asked?

66

WHEN PEOPLE WALK AWAY FROM GOD

 Begin with prayer

 Read **Jude 5—16**

 Listen at *TTB.org/Jude* to ***Jude 4—6, Jude 6—7, Jude 8—9, Jude 9—11, Jude 11—13,*** and ***Jude 13—16***

One of the most tragic things people and churches and movements can do is walk away from God. That's what it means to have *apostasy from faith*. Jude describes three groups of people who became apostate, who rejected the truth, and then three individuals who walked away from God.

Remember when Israel wandered in the wilderness for 40 years? The reason they never made it to the Promised Land was that they refused to believe God. They wouldn't trust that God would bring them into the land and preferred to stay in the wilderness rather than believe Him. They departed from the faith and died and were buried in that hot sand.

The second group's rebellion happened before the Bible's timeline—when the celestial intelligences, angels, refused to worship God. God created angels with a free will and they refused God's purpose for them. Their rebellion landed some of them in chains, and other fallen angels (demons, apparently) have freedom of movement and today are under Satan's leadership. These spiritual beings will be judged someday, likely during the Millennium. And although we were created lower than the angels, someday we will have part in their judgment (see 2 Peter 2:4).

The third group Jude describes as departed from the faith were the people of Sodom and Gomorrah, who were given over to homosexuality or sodomy. God judged these cities definitively and completely because the people defiled their flesh. Today their ruins are buried beneath the Dead Sea. This is a clear and compassionate warning to our generation.

Those are the three groups of people who became apostate, who rejected the truth. Now Jude warns us of three individuals. First are apostate teachers who "crept in unnoticed," that is, they came in the church's side door pretending to be something they were not.

Here are three ways to identify apostate teachers.

First, they're dreamers; they live in an unreal world. It's nice to think we can solve all our problems by positive thinking, but it's not reality.

Secondly, they "defile the flesh." They engage in base and abnormal immorality. This is the same as the "strange flesh" in the cities of Sodom and Gomorrah that he talked about earlier. Many churches today have gone on record that they approve of homosexuality, but remember God judged the cities of Sodom and Gomorrah. It is not a new morality. There's nothing new about it. It goes back to the days of Noah. These kinds of teachers are dangerous and ungodly. They turn God's grace into carnality.

Third, apostate teachers reject authority and disrespect dignities. They protest against rules and those in authority and might take it out on authority, government, or others in high places. Even Jesus Christ was betrayed from the inside, not the outside. One of His own betrayed Him over to His nation, His nation betrayed Him over to the Romans, and the Romans brought Him to the Cross. The church is being betrayed today by the ones who crept in by the side door.

We learn a lesson about authority from Jude's account of Michael the archangel, arguing with Satan over Moses' body. Satan is a fallen creature and an avowed enemy of God, yet Michael wouldn't bring a sentence that would scorn Satan's dignity. Interestingly, Michael respected Satan's position. Lucifer apparently was the highest creature God created, but then he chose to pitch his will against God's will. He was lifted up by pride, and wanted to become independent of God. He actually thought he could dethrone God—at least from part of His universe. As far as this world is concerned, God has permitted him to carry on this rebellion because God has a high and holy purpose in it. But this creature still believes he will be able to take a segment of God's created universe and be the ruler over it. Satan wants this earth as his.

Yet Michael didn't curse Satan. All he did was say, "The Lord rebuke you," meaning, *"God will take care of you."* He entrusted Satan to God but respected Satan's position as the highest creature created. Michael the archangel teaches us quite a lesson.

A great many believers haven't learned this lesson. Many refuse to bow even to God. We are His creatures; He is our Creator. What right have we to question anything He does? God is also our Redeemer, the One who loves us. But our God is high, holy, and lifted up. He is just and righteous. He never makes any mistakes nor does anything wrong. Everything He does is right and, therefore, we can trust Him. But do we? Do we respect His authority? Do we respect His person? In that day when we will give an account, the Lord Jesus Christ is going to say, *"You said, 'Lord, Lord,' but you didn't do the things I commanded. Each one went his own way and did that which was right in his own eyes"* (see Matthew 7:23). This is the picture of mankind. How about you?

Finally, those who reject God, the apostates, sneer at anything they can't understand, and by doing whatever they feel like doing—living by animal instinct only—they participate in their own destruction.

Jude uses two words here that both translate to "know." They "speak evil of whatever they *do not know;* and whatever they *know naturally,* like brute beasts, in these things they corrupt themselves."

The first "know" speaks of "mental comprehension and knowledge." We know some things because we put them in a test tube or look at them under a microscope. But you can't know the finer things of life this way. Think of a wonderful piece of music. Music needs to be translated into sound, and the ear needs to hear it—you can't see it at all; it's invisible. Love is also invisible and so is faith. We know a great many things without any proof from the laboratory. We know them because we've experienced them. The Holy Spirit has made them real to our hearts.

The second word Jude uses for "know" means "to understand." Originally this kind of "know" implied being skilled in tangible things, things you can see and handle. These are things you *can* pour into the test tube and things that brute beasts know by instinct. Like the ducks in Canada, vacationing there for the summer, one day take off and head south. By instinct, they know that soon snow will fall and the lake will freeze. They move like beasts do, by instinct. They don't understand or comprehend knowledge.

The apostates who fancy themselves as smart because they only believe what they can prove in a test tube are a poor generation. They don't understand anything more than by animal instinct. They've not reached the higher plane of knowledge. Knowing just physical things, they think they know everything that can be known, and they corrupt themselves in these things.

This is the picture of the apostates that Jude paints for us. The apostasy that was a cloud the size of a man's hand is now a raging storm lashing across the church, casting up foam and fury. We need to hang out this epistle as a storm warning, because apostasy is in our churches today.

Jude cries one word over them—"Woe!" It's a wail of sorrow and denunciation.

He shares this sorrow by showing us three illustrations. The first is "the way of Cain," which describes an apostate as someone who is religious yet denies they are a sinner. If he denies that he is a sinner, then he also denies the redemption available to him in Christ Jesus. Remember Cain, Adam and Eve's boy? He refused to bring a lamb as Abel did (see Hebrews 11:4). The way of Cain is the way of a religious man who refuses to follow God's specific command. In other words, he didn't come to God by faith; he didn't believe God when He said man was to bring a sacrifice and that without shedding of blood there's no forgiveness of sins, that the penalty must be paid. Cain just didn't believe any of that. He didn't recognize he was a sinner. Abel wasn't better than Cain, but he knew he was a sinner needing God to save him, and he came by faith.

Another illustration of this rebellion is Balaam. Balaam was all about the money, and it was his undoing. He was a hired preacher who wanted to make a buck from his God-given gift. He said nice things because people wanted to hear nice things. God rebuked the prophet with biting sarcasm. The donkey Balaam was riding on spoke to Balaam, but when Balaam got the message, he didn't heed it. Instead, he turned from God. Other apostates have been greedy for things other than just money. Some craved prominence, popularity, fame, applause, and position. This is all the way of Balaam.

Next, Jude used a story from Moses' lifetime as another illustration of an apostate. A man named Korah led a rebellion against Moses in Numbers 16 because he thought Moses believed he was the only one who had access to God. In reality, Korah rebelled against God's authority, represented by Moses. He intruded into a sacred thing. *"Who does Moses think he is?"* The truth was, Moses didn't think too much of himself and wanted to disqualify himself as the leader out of Egypt, but God had called him. When Korah rebelled against Moses, God took Korah out. He was a rebellious man rebelling against God—just like the apostates.

Jude described these three Old Testament rebels to illustrate what it looks like to be an apostate. Cain didn't believe you needed to come to God by faith and needed a bloody sacrifice because man's a sinner. He just believed if you had a religion, that was enough. Balaam's mistake was thinking sinners couldn't be forgiven—that what God requires isn't enough. That Jesus' sacrifice isn't enough. And Korah's error was to assume an authority that wasn't his. These are all examples of apostates.

Jude then goes on to describe modern apostate teachers in vivid, graphic, dramatic, and frightening language. He says apostates are like a hidden reef that rips up ships. They're like shepherds feeding themselves and not their sheep. They're like clouds with no rain and trees with no fruit. They know how to spiritualize a text of Scripture and make it mean something entirely different than what God intended it to mean. They look like they're filled with the Word of God, but they're empty and dry. Beautiful clouds that pass over. They're like "wandering stars" through space, lawless, following no course whatsoever—in "the blackness of darkness forever," like someday in eternal punishment. How frightful!

Jude then shares something fascinating. He quotes a prophecy from Enoch, a man who lived before Noah's time. Enoch walked with God (see Genesis 5:24),and God removed Enoch from this earthly scene without him dying. Enoch left a record that was known to the early church fathers of the second century, but which God apparently didn't want in the canon of Scripture or it would be there. But this one prophecy Enoch made concerning the coming of Christ with His saints, God wanted to put into the record of His Word.

Enoch's prophecy talks about God's saints; they will be removed from the earth—some without dying—and caught up to meet the Lord in the air. This Rapture is the next thing on God's agenda and it is translated "an apostasy." Just like an apostasy is a departure from the faith, the Rapture is a departure of the true church from the earth. We will return with Jesus Christ at the Second Coming—but to "execute judgment on all," to convict all who are destitute of reverential awe towards God.

When you read "ungodly" apostates, think of people who just leave God out. They don't have a reverential awe of Him. They murmur and complain and leave God out of everything. If they recognize God at all, they blame Him for everything bad that has happened to them. They walk after their own desires. They want what they want. They also talk with "great swelling words" that are like the waves of the ocean—lots of fizz and foam, but no content. They compliment each other, applauding and saying a lot of things that are not true because they hope to get promoted and praised (see James 2:1-4).

This is how you can spot an apostate. They don't look to God. They don't even think about whether or not the Lord Jesus will say to them, "Well done, good and faithful servant" (Matthew 25:21). They are more concerned with having the applause of the crowd. Now that you know what to look for, you'll see them everywhere.

NEXT: How do we live in a world of fake religion?

LESSON 2
♥ FOR DISCUSSION AND REFLECTION

1. It is easy to feel like we would never abandon our faith, but what can the examples Jude gives tell us about that possibility in our lives?

2. Given Jude's description of the characteristics of false teachers, how can you be on the alert for them?

3. Are there any subtle ways you maybe haven't consistently respected God's authority in your life?

4. Knowledge is good, but sometimes our knowledge can be part of the problem. We don't always know what we think we know, and we never know what God knows. How does your attitude toward knowledge, and what you think you know, need to be changed by the Holy Spirit?

5. We can all agree that false teachers are bad, but the truly difficult part is examining our own lives to see if we exhibit some of their same behaviors, even if we continue in the Christian faith. Are there any places in your life where you are deceitful? Are there places where your love for God and His people is not genuine? Are there places where you have refused to let the Holy Spirit rule in your life?

6. What does the prophecy of Enoch tell us about God and His plans for His people?

7. If you had been a companion of Jude, what questions would you have had for him about dealing with false teachers?

GOD LOVES YOU,
AND HE WANTS TO GIVE YOU
THAT PEACE SO THAT AT NIGHT
YOU CAN PILLOW YOUR HEAD
ON HIS PROMISES.
THRU the BIBLE

HOW TO LIVE IN A BROKEN WORLD

 Begin with prayer

 Read **Jude 17—25**

 Listen at *TTB.org/Jude* to *Jude 16—19, Jude 19—20,* and *Jude 20—25*

Now that we're certain we live in a world that denies Jesus Christ as Lord, and likely this apostasy is already present in our churches and Christian communities today, the apostle Jude tells us how believers can live in a broken world.

First, we shouldn't let this "falling away" disturb us. God has permitted it for a purpose.

Then, Jude turns from describing the apostates and talks directly to believers in saying, "But you, beloved ...," meaning beloved of God. *"Remember God's Word; remember what Jesus Christ taught us."*

All through Scripture we're told to remember God's Word. When we know the Bible, we can call it up when we need to be reminded of God's great truths. You can't stand for God without tripping up unless you know God's Word for yourself.

Jude reminds us that in the last times, mockers will walk after their own ungodly lusts. Their desires are totally apart from God and from the will of God. These apostates treat spiritual things like a joke and make a religion out of their own whims and lusts. There's no sign of the Spirit at work in their lives at all.

How do you know when someone is sincere in their relationship with the Lord? You can use the Word of God like a Geiger counter. When you give it out to people, get a response, and watch it revolutionize their lives, you know these people know the Lord. But unregenerate people think you're crazy for believing God and His Word. The Geiger counter doesn't move at all when it's held up against their lives. These apostate unbelievers are the ones who cause divisions in the church. They draw a line through the church, dividing one group against another.

These apostates are "sensual"—the word from which we get the word "psychology." These people live a life centered around themselves. It's an egotistical, selfish way to live—"I come first." But it's a natural way to live for the person who is not born again. The natural man gets all he can for himself—food, money, favor. He lives entirely for himself. They don't have the Holy Spirit living in them.

We as humans have a threefold nature—spirit, soul, and body (see 1 Thessalonians 5:23). In the account of creation, we learn how man was taken from the ground. Did you know that about 15 elements in the dirt are found in our bodies? When we get through with our bodies at death, we move out of them, and the body returns back to the earth. At the resurrection of the believer, the body will be raised a spiritual body. It is sown in corruption, and will be raised in incorruption (see 1 Corinthians 15:42).

Man is also a soul. This word is often misunderstood. Man has a psychological nature in which he relates to the universe and to other souls. In our natural state, we can have charisma and generosity and so much individuality. Everyone can be like this on the surface, though we they are very different underneath.

Above the psychological, God also breathed into us the breath of life, or the spirit. It is that which looks to God, that which longs for God, that which wants to worship.

Man is a trinity: The body or the physical side, the soul or the psychological side, and the spirit or the pneumatic side.

Think of mankind in our three-fold nature as a house with three floors. On the first floor is the dining room and the kitchen—that is the physical. On the second floor is the library and the music room—that is the psychological. On the top floor is a chapel, a place to worship—that is the spiritual. On the top floor is also the Word of God, because man will not understand it without the Spirit of God leading him; the natural man would not even want it.

When Adam chose to sin, the house turned upside down. The spiritual was on the top floor, but at the Fall man died spiritually, and the physical side got up on top. Man today in his natural state is primarily physical. Meat and potatoes are top priority. Self-preservation is the first law of life. But man also enjoys music and loves beauty. He indulges in immorality. This is the sensual part of man that Jude talks about here.

At the Fall, when the spiritual part of man died, he no longer had a capacity for God; in fact, he was now an enemy of God. That is why, when we trust Christ as Savior, we are given a new nature that can respond to the Holy Spirit. Our old nature is still active, too, and we gravitate to fulfilling fleshly desires. (See Romans 8 for more on this.) The natural man is only interested in the things of the flesh, but they who are after the Spirit want to please God. Both now and forever, if you pursue sin, it leads to death. You have no fellowship with God. You can't bring that old nature into obedience to God. You cannot reform man. But a healthy spiritual wellbeing comes from walking with God, and the one who lives in the Spirit and attempts to please God is truly living it up. Instead of going downward and doing the things the flesh wants to do, he can do what God wants done. You can only please Him when you yield to Him and come to the place where He can use you.

Before our conversions, we were dead in our sins. We could walk around, we were physically alive, but we were spiritually dead. When we hear the gospel, the Spirit of God applies it to our hearts, and we trust Christ. That's what it means to be born again. The spiritual nature is reborn, and we now have a capacity for God. But this new nature has no power of its own. So the Holy Spirit comes to dwell in us. The indwelling Spirit is the mark that you are a child of God. He regenerates you. (See John 3:8.) The Holy Spirit is there not only to help you but also to interpret the Word of God to you. The Word of God no longer sounds like foolishness to you, because a new world and a new life have been opened to you.

Every believer has two natures. The old nature, the psychological part of man, wants to turn away from God. The spiritual part now wants to turn to God. If you are a child of God, you know about this conflict. Most of us are like a roller coaster in our Christian lives. We go up today, and it is great, but then we go down tomorrow. The flesh pulls man down and the Spirit pulls man up. You can tell whether or not you are living in the flesh or by the Spirit by looking at what your life produces. See Galatians 5:19-23 for a list. The apostate only can produce the lust of the flesh because he doesn't have the Spirit of God.

Psalm 139:14 says we are "fearfully and wonderfully made," and it's true that man is a complicated creature. We walk around today with a body taken out of the dirt, but we also have a capacity for God. When we become a child of God through faith in Jesus Christ, we want to worship and serve God.

So what can believers do when apostasy invades the church?

1. "Building yourselves up on your most holy faith." "Your most holy faith" doesn't refer to your own personal faith, rather it is *the* faith, the body of truth which has been given to us in the Word of God. You must *study* the Word of God. Study all of it, not just your favorite books. All Scripture is given by inspiration of God. The best thing you can do to prepare for apostasy is to do your best to present yourself to God as one who can rightly handle the word of truth (see 2 Timothy 2:15). Root yourself deep into good, rich soil. When the heat of apostasy burns, you'll be able to stand.

2. "Praying in the Holy Spirit." This means we pray by means of the Holy Spirit; we are dependent on Him. He helps us pray. We don't know what to pray for, so He intercedes for us. (See also Ephesians 6:17-18.)

3. "Keep yourselves in the love of God." God *loves* the believer. Jude addresses the believers as "beloved," as in beloved of *God*. You cannot keep God from loving you, although you can put up an umbrella or a roof so that you will not feel the warmth of God's love. Jude is saying, *"Keep yourselves out there in the sunshine of God's love."* Let His love flood your heart and life. We need this in days of apostasy.

4. "Looking for the mercy of our Lord Jesus Christ unto eternal life." The original word for "looking" means "to expect, to wait for." The Lord Jesus wants us to live in an attitude of expectation for His return.

5. "And have mercy on some, who are doubting." Many sincere people today live in doubt. Be patient with them.

6. "But others save with fear, pulling them out of the fire" refers to sinners whom we consider hopeless. It seems impossible they will ever be saved. Yet if you look around your church, you'll meet some of these people who are now loving and following God. Don't give up on what God may be doing with people. No one is beyond redemption if they want to be saved. Jude encourages us to snatch people out of the fire and have mercy on people.

7. "Hating even the garment defiled by the flesh." The word "flesh" refers to the psychological part of man that can go only so far but cannot be acceptable to God. Everything we do in the flesh is repulsive to God; He *hates* it. And *we* should learn to hate it, too.

This little Epistle of Jude closes with a glorious benediction:

> *Now to Him who is able to keep you from stumbling, and to present you faultless before the presence of His glory with exceeding joy, to God our Savior, who alone is wise, be glory and majesty, dominion and power, both now and forever. Amen.*
> –Jude 24-25

If you want to know the place that Jesus Christ should have in your life, especially in these days of apostasy, memorize this marvelous benediction. As you ponder this blessing, consider the phrase, "through Jesus Christ our Lord." Jesus is God and wants to be Lord of our lives. Give Him glory. Tell others how great He is, how wonderful He is, how mighty He is, and mighty to save. All power is given to Him in heaven and in earth. And before Him someday, you will bow the knee.

In these days of apostasy, God's children can bring glory to the name of Jesus Christ and hold Him up before a denying world.

♥ FOR DISCUSSION AND REFLECTION

1. What, for you personally, is the most challenging part of living in a broken world?

2. Do other believers falling away from the faith affect you? If so, how?

3. If the apostate lives according to their desires, what does the believer in Jesus Christ live according to?

4. The Word of God is not intended to be merely read, but to be lived out in the power of the Holy Spirit. Where are you the weakest when it comes to knowing God's Word and allowing the Spirit to live it out through you?

5. Often, we don't even realize we are living a life that revolves around ourselves, and we need other people to help us see this. Is there someone in your life that can do this for you? If not, who can you ask to help you in this area?

6. Building up is a team activity, not one that is best for individuals. What believers do you know who you can and should build up to help encourage them and protect from apostasy?

7. If you could go back to the first century and talk to Jude, do you think
    he would know that his letter would still be important 2,000 years
    later? What other advice do you think he might give for living the
    Christian life?

THRU THE BIBLE APP

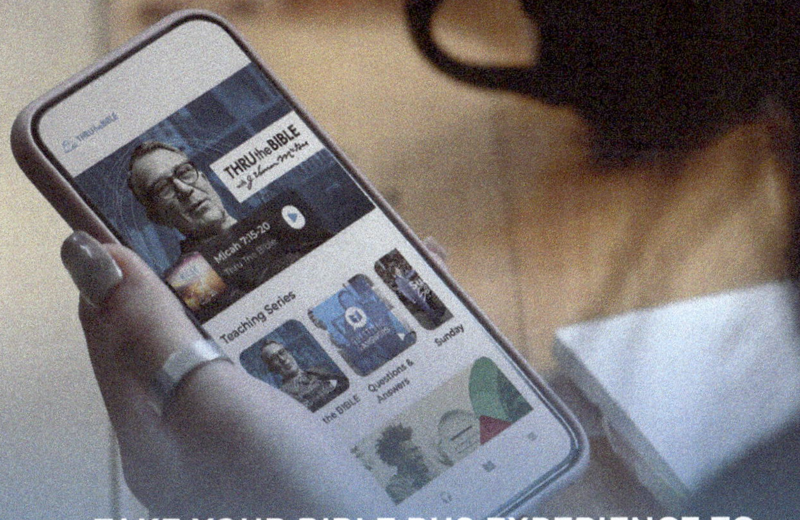

TAKE YOUR BIBLE BUS EXPERIENCE TO THE NEXT LEVEL WITH DR. J. VERNON MCGEE— ALL IN ONE PLACE ON THE APP.

FEATURES YOU'LL LOVE:

LISTEN: Study through the whole Bible, right at your fingertips

TRACK: Personalize your journey by tracking your progress

ACCESS: Download studies for offline engagement

GROW: Enjoy free resources like Notes & Outlines or Bible Companions

SHARE: Tell us about your Bible Bus experience right from the app

SCAN THE QR CODE TO GET THE APP TODAY!

Available in English and a growing list of languages.
Explore all our study apps at *TTB.Bible*.

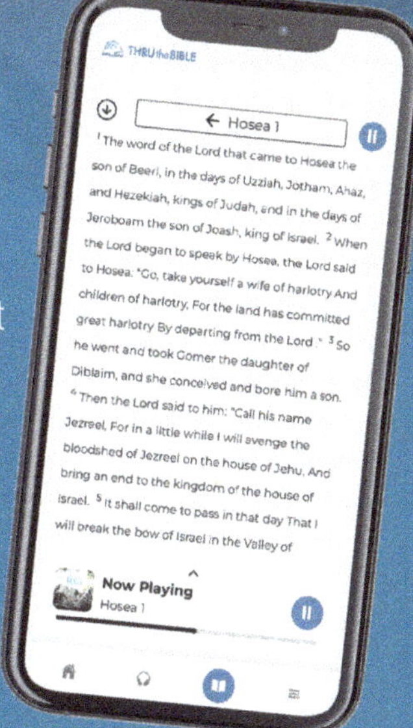

Available in the Apple and Google Play Stores